DRAW A COMIC!

JP Coovert

:01

First Second
New York

Making comics is fun. But comics-related injuries are not!

Be extra careful when using craft knives, scissors, and staplers. If you're using a sharp tool for the first time, ask an adult to show you how to use it safely. Keep your fingers out of the way while cutting and stapling. Trust me, it can really hurt!

Keep your drawing area neat and clean. And be sure to store your tools in a safe place where they can't poke or slice you when you reach for them.

It might not seem like it, but drawing comics can be hard on your body. Comics take a long time to make, and if you spend too much time sitting in one spot drawing, your muscles can get sore and achy. Try not to hunch over your drawings or hold your pencils and pens too tight. Give your eyes a rest every thirty minutes, especially if you're working on a computer. And if you stand up and stretch every so often, your body will thank you for it!

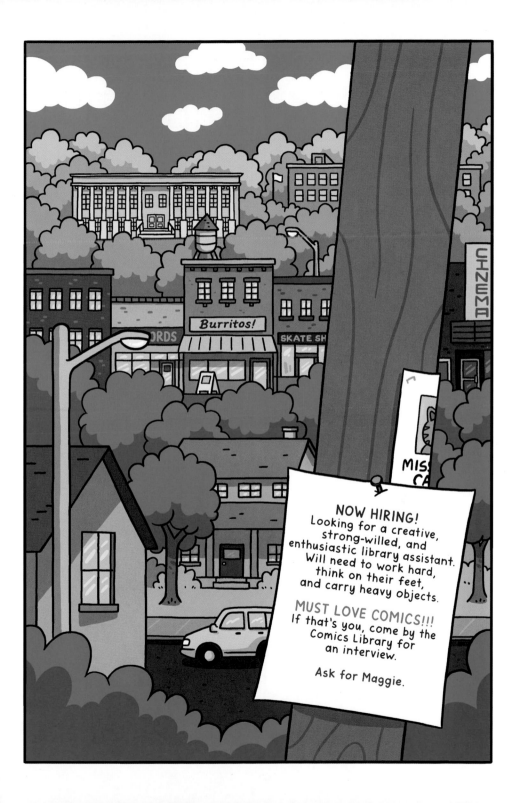

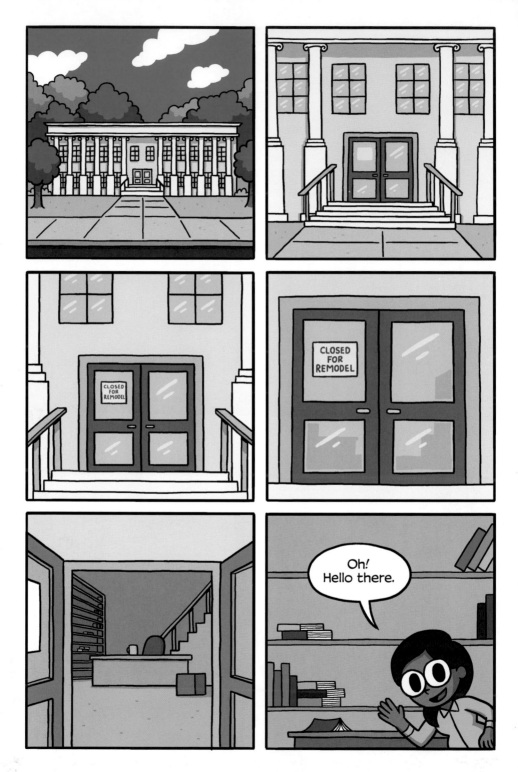

I know it doesn't look like much, but once we are done rebuilding, it will be the largest collection of comics in *the world!*

We have a lot of work to do.

Yes, we do! That's why I need an assistant to help us rebuild!

Now, let's talk qualifications. Number one requirement for this position: You must love comics.

You do love comics, right?

Of course you do! What's not to love?

My grandpa Ollie was the one who shared his love of comics with me. I remember when I was a little girl sitting on his lap while he read the Adventures of Tintin to me.

Ollie Anderson

His lifelong dream was to build a library to share comics with everyone.

Ollie Anderson

9

And this is a **thought balloon**. They indicate when a character is thinking something. Notice the little bubbles? They point to who is doing the thinking.

Could it be? A friendy T. rex?

What about this box, Maggie?

65 million years ago...

That's a **caption**. They are boxes with text in them. Captions can explain lots of different things, like the time and place.

They can represent the voice of a narrator.

The T. rex was a fierce hunter.

Or they can be used for off-panel dialogue. Adding quotation marks makes it clear you're quoting someone who's not there.

"What's up, Triceratops?"

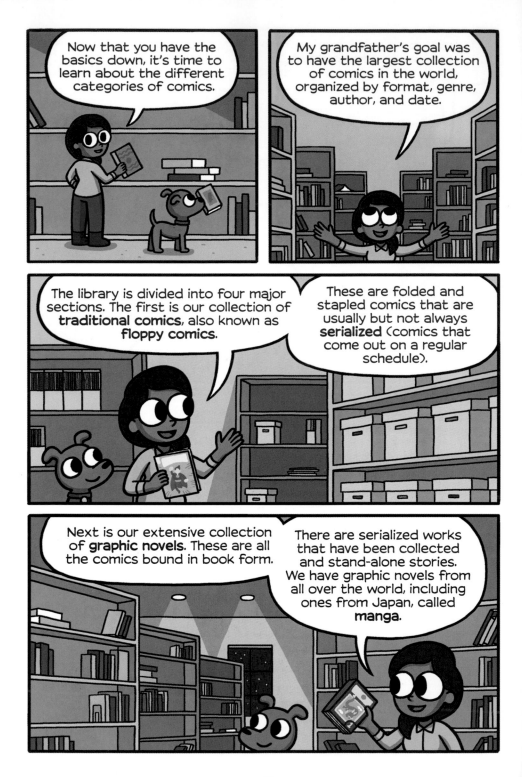

Now that you have the basics down, it's time to learn about the different categories of comics.

My grandfather's goal was to have the largest collection of comics in the world, organized by format, genre, author, and date.

The library is divided into four major sections. The first is our collection of **traditional comics**, also known as **floppy comics**.

These are folded and stapled comics that are usually but not always **serialized** (comics that come out on a regular schedule).

Next is our extensive collection of **graphic novels**. These are all the comics bound in book form.

There are serialized works that have been collected and stand-alone stories. We have graphic novels from all over the world, including ones from Japan, called **manga**.

25

PROJECT TWO: PLANNING A COMIC STRIP

The next morning

Assistant! Right on time. Follow us back to the garage, and I'll tell you about your next project.

We are going to write and draw an original comic strip!

All you'll need is a few sheets of paper and a pencil.

What is a **comic strip** exactly?

A comic strip is a short—usually only a few panels—comic that often ends with a punch line. They became popular in the 1890s. Not long after that, they were printed every day in newspapers.

Every day?! That seems like a lot of work!

That is a lot, Rex. But we are going to start simple and just make one, like this.

What are you doing after work, Maggie?

Hmm. I think I'll go on an adventure!

Later...

The first step when creating your own comic is to come up with a story.

My best advice is to write about something you know. Maybe it's a comic about something that happened to you once. A trip you went on or something funny you saw. Maybe you can tell a story about an adventure you and your friends went on.

And don't be afraid to use your imagination! You can tell any kind of story you want with comics!

My comic strip is going to be about a dog who finds a hidden treasure!

So you have an idea? The second step is to write a **script**.

Since we are writing **and** drawing the comic strip ourselves, let's move on to the next step, **thumbnails**.

But I don't have thumbs...

No, not the kind on your fingers; these are the next phase of the plan. Thumbnails are little, quick, sketchy drawings used to plan out how your comic will look.

You figured out all the words in the "script" phase. Now it's time to make sure the drawings and the words work well together.

Take a piece of scrap paper, and sketch out your panel borders with a pencil.

Now follow your script and loosely sketch in your characters, narration, word balloons, and sound effects so they don't crowd each other.

Don't spend too much time on this part. You can even use stick figures to keep it quick. There's no need to draw the thumbnails really big, either. Draw them at a size that feels comfortable and is still legible.

31

*Close-up, establishing shot, and medium shot are terms that were first used by filmmakers. Comics and film share some of the same concepts and terminology.

There are also **non-photo blue** pencils.

They are a light blue color that, when scanned into a computer or photo copier, show up very light, so it's easy to remove the pencil marks from your artwork.

A lot of cartoonists like these because they don't have to erase after inking.

More on this later!

All these rules apply to mechanical pencils, as well.

But with mechanical pencils, you have to pay attention to the thickness of the graphite, too, which is measured in millimeters. When you're shopping for refills, the size of the graphite and the pencil have to match.

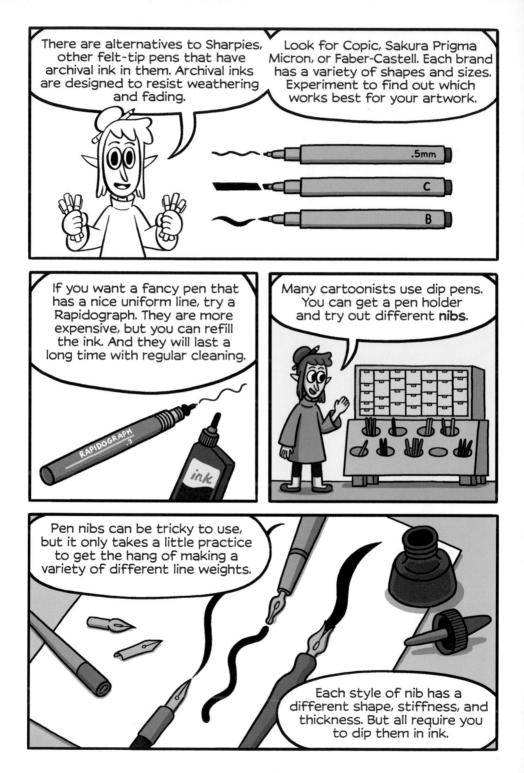

There are alternatives to Sharpies, other felt-tip pens that have archival ink in them. Archival inks are designed to resist weathering and fading.

Look for Copic, Sakura Prigma Micron, or Faber-Castell. Each brand has a variety of shapes and sizes. Experiment to find out which works best for your artwork.

.5mm

C

B

If you want a fancy pen that has a nice uniform line, try a Rapidograph. They are more expensive, but you can refill the ink. And they will last a long time with regular cleaning.

RAPIDOGRAPH .3

ink

Many cartoonists use dip pens. You can get a pen holder and try out different nibs.

Pen nibs can be tricky to use, but it only takes a little practice to get the hang of making a variety of different line weights.

Each style of nib has a different shape, stiffness, and thickness. But all require you to dip them in ink.

A similar option is using a brush. There are synthetic and natural hair versions that range in price. Both types have benefits and drawbacks.

Every brush has a different size indicated by a number.

BRUSHES

The smaller the number, the smaller the tip of the brush.

There is also a variety of brush shapes.

ROUND

#0 #2 #6   FLAT FILBERT CHISEL

A good place to start is a size 2 round brush.

Just like pen nibs, brushes need to be dipped in ink.

Don't cover all the brush bristles in ink though, just the tip.

The tools you choose to draw with will determine what type of paper you will need.

If you are working with a simple HB pencil and ballpoint pen, then maybe just plain white copy paper will do. The important thing is that the paper is white and doesn't have any lines on it.

Cartoonists who use nibs and brushes often choose to work on bristol board. It's a thicker paper that won't scratch or bleed when ink is applied.

BRISTOL BOARD

There are different textures, like smooth or vellum, which has a slightly rough texture. Try out different kinds with your favorite tools to see what you like best.

Smooth   Vellum

There's also transparent vellum, which is a high-quality kind of tracing paper.

ELLUM

Some cartoonists use this type of paper if they don't want to ink directly on top of their pencils. But be careful: This paper is fragile and prone to wrinkling.

Two generations of Anderson originals? You got yourself a deal!

Thank you so much, Momo! The pieces fit together perfectly.

Where do we go next, Maggie?

Floyd's! Let's go to the comic shop, Rex!

We gotta pay first.

Of course, the supplies will set us back a bit but are worth it for all the awesome comics we are going to make!

I can't wait to read them.

See you there!

Thank you for everything, Momo!

With a pencil, lightly sketch out a few words to get an idea of how tall the words will be. Then use your ruler to measure the height.

sniff

Using the height of your letters, measure out several horizontal lines in each panel. Draw the lines lightly so they'll be easy to erase later.

sniff

Be sure to add space in between each line. Usually half the height of your letters is good.

snif

After your guides are drawn, carefully pencil in all of the text in your comic strip.

Then draw narration boxes and word and thought balloons around the text.

sniff
sniff

dig
dig

I'm rich!

Remember! Don't fill up the entire panel with the text, or you won't have space for the drawings.

Now comes the really fun part. Pencil in the characters.

Using a pencil, sketch out the drawings of your comic strip. We will ink over these drawings later to finalize them, so don't worry about being clean and perfect. This is meant to be a planning stage.

sniff sniff

dig dig

I'm rich!

What if my characters are looking kinda lifeless?

Don't worry if the drawings aren't just right. The reason we are using pencil is so we can erase, too!

The trick to drawing good characters is figuring out how to make their expressions and poses obvious, so the reader can tell exactly how the characters are feeling and what they are doing.

Let's talk about expression first. Ask yourself, "How is this character feeling in this panel?"

Are they happy? Angry? Sad? Surprised?

Determined!

These backgrounds are complicated and hard to draw. Do I need to have a background in every panel?

Not always! Sometimes all you need is an establishing shot. Show the background in the first panel to set up where the characters are located.

Then you can just draw simple indications that they are in the same space.

Backgrounds can also help explain when characters are moving from one space...

...to another.

Backgrounds are also a great indicator of the time of day in comics.

Okay! I get it now. Backgrounds really add a lot to the story, too!

*More info on scanning in the glossary.

This time we are going to draw the artwork larger, then learn how to scale it down.

A lot of professional cartoonists draw bigger because little mistakes disappear when the artwork is scaled down for printing.

Drawing smaller and scaling up can decrease the quality of your artwork, though, so we aren't going to do that.

I like to draw my comics 1.5x the regular scale, or at 150 percent.

We know that your comic pages will be printed at 5.5 x 8.5 inches or a piece of letter paper folded in half, right?

So that means we just need to multiply those dimensions by 1.5. So the scaled-up dimensions will be 8.25 x 12.75 inches.

artwork size

print size

12.75"

8.25"

Let's call these dimensions the **page border**. No artwork should ever go outside of it.

12.75"

8.25"

Now take out your pencil and the 11- x 14-inch (or bigger) drawing paper.

Ready!

Using your ruler and T square, draw out the 8.25- x 12.75-inch page border.

We don't want the artwork to go up to the very edge of the paper, so we need to add a **margin**, or extra space, inside the page border.

page border

margin

Measure out a .75-inch margin *inside* the page border.

.75"

.75"

.75"

.75"

When we reduce the size of the artwork later, the margin will scale down to .5 inches.

.75"

.5"

Plenty of space so the copier won't cut off the artwork.

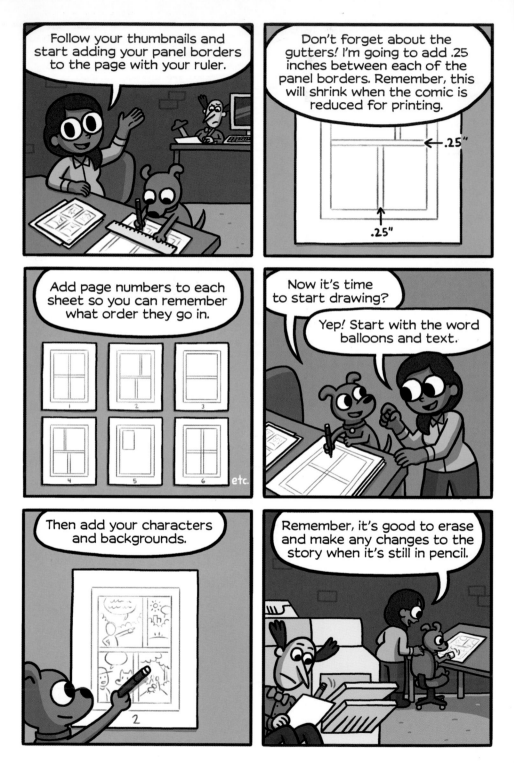

Just align one of your original pages on a photocopier. Use the copier's interface to adjust the scale.

Since we did the original art at 150 percent, scale it down 66 percent to get it back to the print-ready size of 5.5 x 8.5 inches, then hit print.

COPY

PAPER 8.5 × 11

SCALE 66%

COPIES 1

PRINT

Do this for every page of artwork, even the covers. Once you have a stack of printed pages, cut the artwork out with your scissors.

Vrrrrr

Now pull out your dummy book, because it's time to lay out your comic.

We need to tape all of your printed pages into their corresponding pages of the dummy book to make a **master copy**. We'll use the master copy to print our comic book from.

clear tape

page 2   page 3

before   after

Once all of your pages have been taped into the dummy book, you should be able to read your entire comic!!!

the end.

119

NOTES ON MEASUREMENTS

TIPS FOR SCANNING

Here's a rundown of how you should scan in artwork, depending on how you drew it.

Black and White or Bitmap

If your ink artwork is only black and white (no shades of gray!), you can scan in this mode. But do it at a really high resolution, like 1200 DPI.

Grayscale

Grayscale mode is for black-and-white artwork that has shades of gray, like pencil or ink wash. Scan in your artwork at 600 DPI in this mode.

Color

If you've made full-color artwork, scan in this mode. 300 DPI is a high enough resolution for color.

This is a glossary of some of the terms we used while working on our comics.

caption—Boxes with words inside them that provide extra info or give voice to a narrator.

close-up—A framing device used to bring attention to a subject by showing its details.

comic strip—Short comic usually ending in a punch line.

dummy book—Guide used to figure out the pagination of a comic book.

emanata—Symbols used to indicate mood or emotion.

establishing shot—Framing method used to show the subject in an environment.

graphic novel—A bound comic in book form.

grid—Arranging panels in a uniform way.

gutter—Space between panels.

margin—Space between comic artwork and the edge of a page.

master copy—The finalized, high-quality mock-up of a comic book used for reproduction.

medium shot—Framing method that shows a subject and background elements.

pagination—The order pages are placed into a signature when printing a comic book.

panel—The boxes with words and pictures that make up a page of a comic.

saddle stitch—Binding method used to create a comic book by folding and stapling signatures.

script—Written plan for a comic.

signature—A single sheet of paper that is folded to create multiple pages of a comic book.

sound effect—Stylized words to indicate sound.

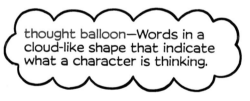

thought balloon—Words in a cloud-like shape that indicate what a character is thinking.

thumbnails—Quick and simple version of a comic used for planning.

traditional comic book—Folded and stapled comic book.

web comic—Comic published on the internet.

word balloon—Words in a circular shape that show a character speaking.

MORE BOOKS TO READ!

And last but not least, I've pulled a bunch of other great books from our collection that have a *ton* of information about creating comics. Check them out!

Understanding Comics and *Making Comics* by Scott McCloud

Drawing Words and Writing Pictures by Jessica Abel and Matt Madden

The Art of Comic Book Writing by Mark Kneece

Drawing Comics Lab by Robyn Chapman

Let's Make Comics! by Jess Smart Smiley

What It Is and *Syllabus* by Lynda Barry

Your Comics Will Love You Back! by Alec Longstreth
(alec-longstreth.com/comics/comics_love)

First Second

Published by First Second
First Second is an imprint of Roaring Brook Press,
a division of Holtzbrinck Publishing Holdings Limited Partnership
120 Broadway, New York, NY 10271
All rights reserved

Don't miss your next favorite book from First Second! For the latest updates go to firstsecondnewsletter.com and sign up for our enewsletter.

Library of Congress Control Number: 2018953658

Paperback ISBN: 978-1-250-15212-1
Hardback ISBN: 978-1-250-15211-4

Our books may be purchased in bulk for promotional, educational, or business use. Please contact your local bookseller or the Macmillan Corporate and Premium Sales Department at (800) 221-7945 ext. 5442 or by email at MacmillanSpecialMarkets@macmillan.com.

First edition, 2019
Edited by Robyn Chapman and Bethany Bryan
Expert consultation by Jon Chad
Cover design by Andrew Arnold and Sammy Savos
Interior book design by Rob Steen
Coloring assistance by Jacie Anderson Coovert

Printed in China by 1010 Printing International Limited, North Point, Hong Kong

Created entirely with a Wacom Cintiq Pro 16 in Adobe Photoshop CC with a variety of brushes.

Paperback: 10 9 8 7 6 5 4 3 2 1
Hardcover: 10 9 8 7 6 5 4 3 2 1